The Snuggie Sutra

The Snuggie Sutra

Lex Friedman

Megan Morrison

🦁 St. Martin's Griffin 🐿 New York

www.stmartins.com

Book design by Rich Arnold

Library of Congress Cataloging-in-Publication Data

Friedman, Lex.
    The snuggie sutra / Lex Friedman and Megan Morrison.—1st ed.
        p. cm.
    ISBN 978-0-312-65267-8
    1. Sex instruction. 2. Blankets—Miscellanea. I. Morrison, Megan. II. Title.
    HQ56.F753 2010
    613.9'6—dc22

                                        2010030124

10 9 8 7 6 5 4 3 2

For Lauren. One day, I hope to write a book I can comfortably dedicate to our children as well, some of whom may or may not be conceived with methods covered in this book. —LF

For my amazing friends, of whom even the most squeamish were always willing to critique my work in painstaking detail. And for my family, especially my mother, who laughed in all the right places. —MM

Contents

Preface

The Snuggie is a blanket with sleeves. But it's also a pop culture icon—an "As-Seen-on-TV" wonder that quickly developed its own cult of awareness. Few of us were asking for a blanket with armholes, but that's because we'd forgotten how to dream.

Of course, once we owned our Snuggies, and could cuddle up with a good book and a blanket and not need to let our arms get chilly, we realized the world had changed for the better. Because if you can suddenly reinvent keeping warm while getting cozy with a great novel, there's no reason you can't reinvent keeping warm while getting cozy with a great lover.

Take a moment to think about the images and sensations that come to mind when you think of the Snuggie. Once you get past the television, infomercials, Chia Pets, and the like, you focus in on the Snuggie's hallmarks: Warmth. Coziness. Pleasure.

In other words, just a stone's throw away from orgasm. (Note: Stone throwing may damage both your Snuggie and your nether regions.)

Now, it's not simple to incorporate a Snuggie into your sex life. It takes patience, practice, and at least average physical dexterity to achieve unparalleled sexual bliss with a sleeved blanket.

Over this book's eight chapters, we'll take you through various forms of Snuggie sex, gently guiding you on a fuzzy and warm sexual awakening. And yes, it'll work even if you bought a damn Slanket.

Introduction

The world of Snuggie intimacy and sex—like a willing lover with sleeved blanket in hand—has much to offer:

Warmth. *Nearly every couple consists of one partner who's always shivering while the other sweats. With* The Snuggie Sutra, *the cooler partner can stay toasty warm while getting it on with the nakeder one.*

Coverage. *We're not all Brad Pitt and Angelina Jolie. We're pudgy. We have stretch marks. We have too much body hair. Wrapping yourself up in a Snuggie can leave the proper body parts exposed, while covering up some of the areas you're a little less comfortable with.*

Protection. *A Snuggie can't protect you the same way a condom can, but it can help prevent an arrest for indecent exposure. If you and your loved one are eager to get it on in public, yet still fear getting caught in flagrante delicto, you simply need to pack a Snuggie for your scandalous tryst.*

Creativity. *Missionary, girl-on-top, and the reverse double helix can get boring after a while. Variety is the spice of sex, and introducing a Snuggie into the mix may be just the dose of cinnamon your bedroom needs.*

In order to get the full benefits of the Snuggie, you need to have the right attitude and tools at your disposal. The keys to satisfying Snuggie sex are as follows:

1. Own a Snuggie
2. Have minimal dignity
3. Keep lots of detergent on hand—maybe a Sham Wow
4. Find a willing partner

That last requirement can prove difficult. Even though you're ready to take the leap into the world of Snuggie sex, your loved one may not be. In fact, he or she may be actively opposed. Use your bedroom eyes, and our unimpeachable arguments below, to deal with this vexing challenge.

First off, if your partner is someone who needs convincing to use a Snuggie in the sack, it's high time you consider a new partner.

That said, there are occasions where more timid lovers need some cajoling before they're ready for sleeved-blanket-based canoodling. Fortunately, Snuggie sex offers numerous benefits to most couples. Memorize the following advantages, and share them with your partner over a romantic meal.

1. Change is good. When you've been with the same partner for a long time, things can get stale; there is more to lovemaking than the missionary position. Dirty talk and sex toys can help, but they often leave us feeling privately shameful. Instead, you can ease into your sexual exploration with the comfort and familiarity of a Snuggie. Add spice to your sex life by changing things up — but in a cozy way.

2. Affordability is hot. Heating bills aren't. Wrapping up in a Snuggie with your loved one isn't just intimate — it's also a cost saver. Staying warm in a blanket beautifully

engineered for sexual escapades will not only bring your heat bill down; it can also help save the environment, if you're into that sort of thing.

3. Stretch both your imagination and your muscles. Snuggie sex isn't just about wrapping up in a blanket and then going back to the familiar old awkward jostling that's come to characterize your sex life. As you journey through *The Snuggie Sutra,* you'll encounter positions that become increasingly physical, aerobic, and seemingly impossible. (Of course, that's how many of us view all sex.) By embracing Snuggie sex, and the physical demands such sex embodies, you'll be adding exercise to your extracurricular activities. Early on, you might enjoy the fact that the Snuggie hides unsightly folds of skin, but when the exertions of Snuggie sex start burning extra calories while you roll in the blanketed hay, that's one advantage you'll no longer need!

Now that you and your partner are both panting and pantsless, it's time to grab your Snuggie, grab your loved one's nether regions, and turn the page. (This is a little easier if you have three hands, or do it sequentially.)

A Note on Genders and Roles

Whether you're gay, straight, or Snuggie-curious, anyone can have Snuggie sex. For ease of writing and reading, we've used "him" and "her" and "he" and "she." Regardless of our pronoun choices, feel assured that *The Snuggie Sutra* is for couples of all orientations.

This is your book; use it as you wish. If you want, buy two copies and edit one, crossing out the gendered pronouns that don't work for your relationship, replacing them with ones that do. Your extra purchase will help fund *The Snuggie Sutra Two: Erotic Bugaloo.*

We want you to have sex in, on, around and through a Snuggie. Who you do it with is up to you.

The
Snuggie
Sutra

Chapter 1

SNUGGIE SEX FOR BEGINNERS: THE MANY TRICKS UP THOSE SLEEVES

You never forget your first time. You explore, feeling your way around soft, welcoming textures you've never encountered. You're bathed in new sensations: Unspeakable warmth, unfamiliar scents, and a feeling of never-before-experienced closeness.

Yes, there's nothing quite like your first time trying on a Snuggie.

And once you've tried on the Snuggie, your mind will quickly turn, wondering what other pleasures you can experience while wrapped in its sleeved, fleecy confines.

The answer, as it often is, is sex.

The basic mechanics of sex with a Snuggie aren't all that different from the mechanics of wearing the Snuggie itself: Find the right holes, and go to town.

These first positions should get both you and your

partner comfortable; you'll get frisky without getting frigid. Even though the positions that follow are some of the easiest ones within *The Snuggie Sutra,* they may take the most time to learn as you prepare your body and mind for incorporating the blanket into your sex. If at first your body parts don't line up the right way (nobody wants a penis in the ear), or if you can't hold certain positions for the entirety of the sex act, don't get discouraged. Like a good lover, be patient, and take whatever comes.

1. The Wraparound Sue

You're both standing, and he wraps his arms
around her. She drapes the Snuggie on her back,
tying the sleeves behind his neck. Keep your
friends close, and your genitals closer.

2. The Booster Seat

He sits on the floor, and she sits on his lap while wearing the Snuggie. With him underneath her, she'll be able to reach *everything* she craves.

3. The Tunnel of Love

Both of you lie down, faceup, atop the open Snuggie. Each of you places your outside arm in a sleeve, and then wrap those sleeved arms around each other. You've formed your own dark nether region—now find each other's.

4. The Manket

The man wears the Snuggie on his back and keeps his partner warm. Perfect for long winter nights, cold winter mornings, and when your partner is sedated.

5. The Warm and Snuggie

You both get in the Snuggie together. The Snuggie can go either way, and with luck, you can convince your partner to do the same.

6. The Roller Coaster

The woman wears the Snuggie on her front and covers him. Hang on tight—it's going to be a bumpy ride!

7. The Cuddly Puppy

The man wears the Snuggie on his front and covers her. She feels warm and cozy like Grandma's house, but still knows who her daddy is.

8. The Tablecloth

The meal was delicious, the guests have gone home, and the table has been cleared. She lies on her back on the table, her legs through the armholes, the bottom of the Snuggie covering her. It's just not a holiday without stuffing.

9. The Dark Horse

Cover yourselves with the Snuggie as a tight, confining tent. The armholes are your sole source of ambient lighting. Good when your partner has a horse face.

10. The Quick and Fuzzy

He wears the Snuggie as she leans against the wall. Wham, bam, you're welcome ma'am.

Chapter 2

WOMAN ON TOP: GOOD FOR FEMINISM, GOOD FOR PLEASURE

When women are empowered, men can feel vulnerable. But once a Snuggie is involved, everyone feels comfortable—provided you're all naked underneath. That's because positions where the woman is on top needn't serve only to make the woman feel powerful.

The man, after all, often must support his woman's weight in these positions. He can thus feel manly while fornicating, which is always a good thing. And let's not forget that men—men who are gentle and sensitive enough to appreciate the warmth that only a blanket with sleeves can provide—can become aroused from the mere act of empowering the women in their lives.

Empowered woman, plus aroused and enlightened man, multiplied by Snuggie, equals hot and sexy Snuggilicious actions.

11. The Red-breasted Cockatoo

The man lies faceup. The woman gets atop him, wearing the Snuggie, flapping her fleece wings as she bounces. It's the most fun you'll ever have bird watching.

12. The Deck Chair

The man lies on his back, with his knees up, his legs through the sleeves. The woman straddles him and lies back, comfortably resting on the folded fabric stretched taut between his legs. The Deck Chair works equally well in the sun or indoors. Don't forget the lotion!*

* Note: Depending on your anatomy, this position may require creating an additional hole in your Snuggie.

13. The Dogsled

The man sits up, and the woman mounts him, wearing the Snuggie on her back. He holds the end of the Snuggie, whipping the reigns to make her go faster. Giddyup!*

* Note: Purists may prefer the dog-sled call, "Mush!"

14. The Shame

The woman wears the Snuggie on her front,
and covers her partner with the bottom. Perfect
for showing off your dominating moves in the
saddle—and when you can't stand to look him
in the eye.

15. The Snuggie Whisperer

The man lies on his side. She wears the Snuggie on her back and reaches around his front. Her lips linger by his ear, whispering sweet nothings while giving him sweet somethings.

16. The Yes Ma'am

The woman wears the Snuggie on her back and keeps her partner warm by wrapping it around his front. Great for hiding your flaws, or when you're doing it on a park bench or subway grate.

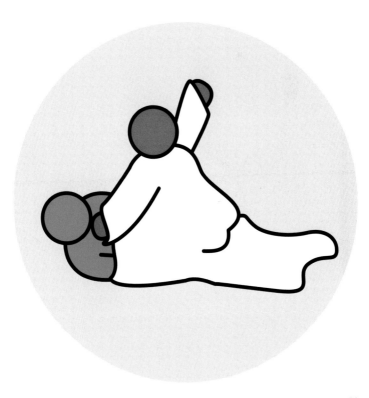

17. The Chaps

The woman faces the man's feet and wears the Snuggie on her back, covering her partner with the rest. She won't miss a minute of *Sex in the City,* and he won't miss the tattoo of her ex's name on her ass.

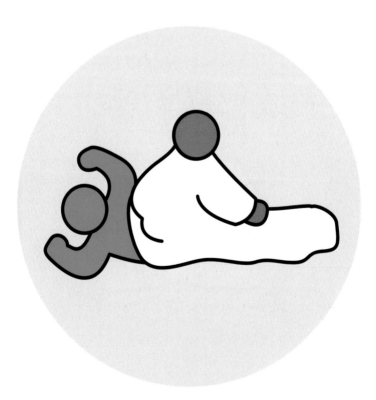

18. The Power Lift

The man lies on his back. The woman squats above him, facing away, wearing the Snuggie on her back. She should stretch first to make sure that she can handle the load.

19. The Luge

She lies on top of him backward as the Snuggie covers both of them. The faster you go, the hotter it gets.

20. The Bow of the Boat

She sets sail on top of him wearing the Snuggie. She is graceful at the helm as he charts a course for Pleasuretown.

Chapter 3

ROLE PLAYING: DRESS UP, THEN GET DOWN

Many of us occasionally wear different hats during sex—sometimes, literally. More often, those hats are strictly metaphorical, as we take on other personas while we get it on. Sexual role-playing can help loosen inhibitions, not to mention rekindle nostalgic memories from drama club.

French maids, naughty schoolgirls, and the like are all fun, and should certainly remain a part of your sexual repertoire. But by introducing the Snuggie into your bedroom fantasies, you'll uncover kinks you never knew you had.

That's because few of us ever really feel at ease in slutty nurse costumes or assless chaps; even if your partner gets aroused, you're wondering whether your butt looks too big, or if this getup is going to chafe.

The Snuggie, with its smooth fabric and all-over coverage, lets you stay extra comfy during your sexual adventures.

21. The Magic Wand

He wears the Snuggie while standing. He may be wearing the cape, but she'll be the one making the magic happen. (Wizard hat optional.)

22. The Drunken Sailor

She's on her back, legs in the air, with her head at the edge of the bed. He operates her legs like the ship's steering wheel. When the rhythm is just right, he can lower his boom.

23. The Hi-Yo Silver

The woman wears the Snuggie on her back, and he holds the bottom. Ride off into the sunset, but all the while you can stay inside where it's nice and warm.

24. The Bucking Bronco

The Snuggie goes on the floor and is used for balance and stability. Lasting for eight seconds does not make you a winner.

25. The Straitjacket

The woman wears the Snuggie on her front, the sleeves tying her arms behind her. Things are going to get crazy.

26. The Dentist's Chair

The patient lies back and relaxes wearing the Snuggie on her front. Open wide so the dentist can get in there nice and deep.

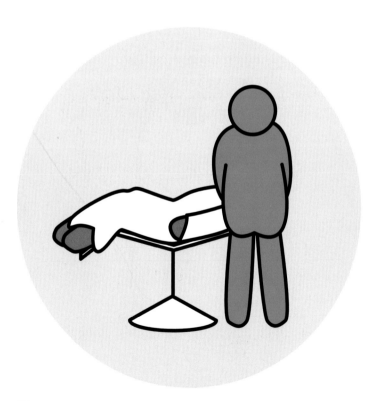

27. The Pony Express

The man sits on a chair. The woman sits on his lap facing the same direction he is. She wears the Snuggie on her back. She will ride as much as she has to in order to deliver her message.

28. The Karate Kid

The man wears the Snuggie like a kimono, practicing his art. She watches while he wax off.

29. The Marge Simpson

She can raise three kids, cook a delicious meal, bail you out of a mess—and she still knows her way around the bedroom. Mmmmmmmmmmmm . . . Marge.

30. The Zorro

He wears the Snuggie as a cape. When a lady is in need, the hero will brandish his weapon and make everything all right.

31. The Cookie Monster

She creates a Cookie Monster–like mouth by grasping a fistful of the Snuggie fabric. You know what "C" is for.

Chapter 4

INTERMEDIATE SNUGGIE SEX: THRUSTING ONWARD

The key to making your sex life fresh: Keep changing things up in the bedroom. The key to making your sex life fantastic: Keep incorporating your Snuggie.

You already know and love positions like the Yes Ma'am (see chapter 2). But it's important to keep finding new positions to enjoy. How important? It's just as important as keeping your Snuggie freshly washed.

The positions are getting harder, and so will he.

32. The Quasimodo

You're both inside the Snuggie, and there's a lot of humping going on.

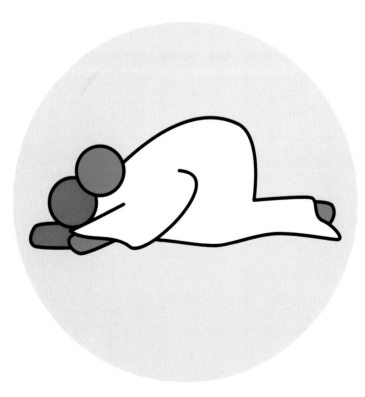

33. The Mighty Mississippi

You both lie down; the one on top wears the Snuggie sleeves. You're makin' waves as you're rollin' down the fleece river.

34. The Director's Chair

He wears the Snuggie across his front, stretching the fabric taut between his legs to form a seat. He'll need to make a new hole in his Snuggie for this to work. She, on the other hand, should already have one.*

* Note: You can use the same Snuggie you doctored for The Deck Chair, page 15.

35. The Papoose

He wears the Snuggie on his back and gathers it around her as he carries her. Lightweight, flexible, and easy to carry anywhere, but right here seems just fine.

36. The Morning Glory

Each of you puts an arm through a sleeve, and the Snuggie covers both of you. You'll love the smell of fresh Snuggie in the morning.

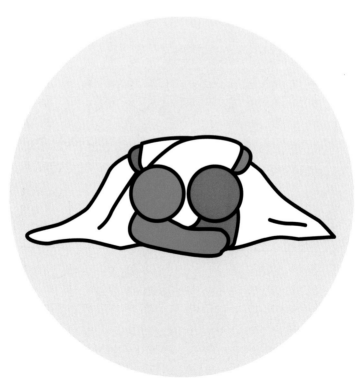

37. The Buffet

She lies down on the table, wearing the Snuggie. This appetizing spread provides plenty of options to choose from, and with luck he'll come back for seconds, and thirds—until you're both satisfied.

38. The Superwoman

She wears the Snuggie on her back. He holds the other end in his teeth. You're super if you can hold yourself up and keep him quiet at the same time.

39. The Pillow Fluffer

The woman stands behind a couch and wears the Snuggie on her front. Cleaning the house never felt so dirty.

40. The Safety Harness

The man sits on the chair. The woman sits on him, facing him. The Snuggie goes on *her* back, but *his* arms are through the sleeves. Safety comes first—and again and again and again.

41. The Loveseat

The man sits backward on a chair wearing the Snuggie on his back, with the woman on his lap, facing him. If you position the chair just right, you'll be sure to optimize his feng shui.

42. The Moby Dick

After years of searching, he will finally find that which has eluded him for so long. He buries his harpoon deep, bringing the tail to its thrilling climax.

43. The Goalposts

Her legs go through the sleeves with the Snuggie draped over his chest. It's up and it's good—very good.

44. The Mantle

Hang the Snuggie up by the chimney with care.
Invite her to come get her stocking stuffed there.
The Snuggie will take on a comforting form—
Even if there's no fire, you'll still both be warm.

Chapter 5

ORAL SNUGGIE SEX: THINKING OUTSIDE THE BOX

Oral sex is fun. If this statement of fact is news to you, put the book down and go find a willing mouth. You've been missing out.

Welcome back. Now that you know the joys of oral pleasure, you may be surprised to learn that there are downsides to going down—which *The Snuggie Sutra* can overcome:

First, there's overexposure. Sometimes, you or your partner may feel vulnerable with your most private parts ready for such up-close-and-personal inspection. When the Snuggie enters the picture, it provides sensuous shadows and tantalizing obfuscation.

And let's not forget that, by its very nature, the Snuggie provides extra warmth, the perfect cure for problems like shrinkage.

You may be shocked to your core to learn oral sex can get even better. *The Snuggie Sutra* makes it happen.

45. The Superfan

He wears the Snuggie while parked in front of the television. Regardless of the score, he still comes out a winner.

46. **The Amuse-Bouche**

He sits on the kitchen counter. Her arms go through the Snuggie, with the bottom covering him. A little palate pleaser to whet your appetite.

47. The *Sechzig-neun*

His arm and her leg go into the Snuggie's holes,
as he stretches across and gets bathed in warmth.
Like the name, it's a real mouthful.

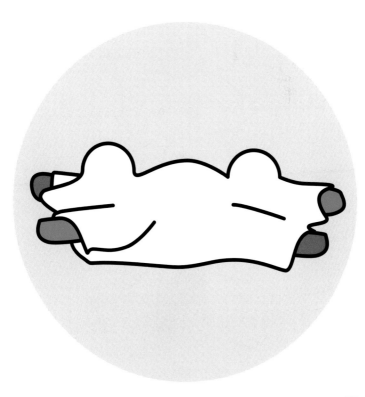

48. The Iceman Cometh

He stands on the "stage" wearing the Snuggie on his back. A great performer knows how to connect with his audience.

49. The Night In

She puts her arms through the sleeves and reads her book. She's minding her own business. He's *also* minding her business.

50. The Late-Night Snack

The woman lies down on the table, draping the Snuggie over her partner's head. It's just the treat to satisfy your hunger in the middle of the night.

51. The Queen of England

She wears the Snuggie like a regal robe, enthroned upon his face. She's royal; they'll both get flushed.

52. The Legs Wide Open

She lies facedown, with her legs wide open, wearing the Snuggie. Her flexibility is sure to bring a smile to his face, but you've got that covered.

53. The Tightrope

He holds the Snuggie, pulled taut. She balances on it, guiding herself up to his mouth. Get your circus freak on.

54. The Old Mother Hubbard

The woman wears the Snuggie on her front while standing. Her cupboard is not bare in this version.

55. The Thank-You

On your last birthday, he gave you a pearl necklace. Now, for his birthday, give him a Snuggie to keep his legs warm—and then let him give you another pearl necklace.

56. The Man-eater

She puts her mouth at the end of one sleeve. Oh, oh, here he comes!

57. The Lunch Date

The woman wears the Snuggie on her front as she sits. It's rude to talk with your mouth full.

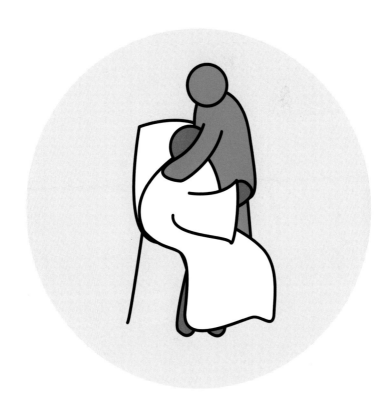

58. The Banana Split

She sits spread-legged on the kitchen counter, and he wears the Snuggie on his back. After a good meal, it's always nice to have something sweet.

59. The Under the Table and Screaming

She wears the Snuggie while seated, and he goes down under the table. Remember, after a really good meal, it's customary to reward excellent service.

69

60. The Silver Platter

He wears the Snuggie on his back and lies on the table. Enjoy gourmet dining in the lap of luxury.

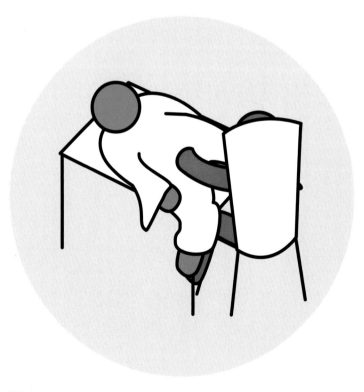

61. The Butterfly Cocoon

The man stands with his legs through the sleeves of the Snuggie holding the ends. The woman waits. When the creature has reached its full size, it emerges from the cocoon in all of its splendor.

Chapter 6

THE MORE THE MERRIER: EXTRA PARTNERS, EXTRA SLEEVES

Don't be scared.

You may think that you'd never consider bringing a third party into your sex lives. But before you bought this book, did you ever think you'd be getting it on while wearing what is, at the end of the day, a soft tieless bathrobe?

To ease you into the idea of "multiples" in the bedroom, not every position in this chapter requires multiple partners. Some just require multiple Snuggies, which are far more willing as lovers.

62. The Snorgy

Go where the mood takes you—and you, and you, and you. If it gets too hot under there, then you're doing it right.

63. The Whole Enchilada

Tie the four sleeves from two Snuggies together. Wrap the three of you inside. The heat inside makes things melt. Delicious.

64. The Window Shade

The males are arranged in a ring around her. Each one wears a Snuggie like a smock. She works her way around the ground, rolling each Snuggie up in turn. There should be no jerks in this circle.

65. The Teepee

She wears one Snuggie on her arms and a second Snuggie on her legs. It's cool in the summer, warm in the winter, and hot all night long.

66. The Wishbone

Two men share one Snuggie (and one woman). With this much going on, someone's wish is coming true.

67. The Tarp

One woman lies on her back. The man, with one arm through the Snuggie, positions himself near her feet. A second woman shares the Snuggie— and more. Even with the proper equipment it will not be easy to stay dry.

68. The Sandwich

The man wears a Snuggie on his back. The woman wears a second Snuggie on her back. It's not important whether it's a six-inch or a twelve-inch; it's the quality of the meat that matters.

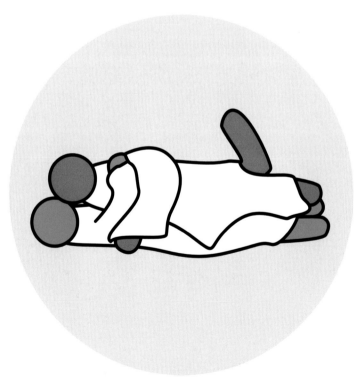

69. The Central Heating

The man lies down and wears one Snuggie on his arms and a second Snuggie on his legs. Experience the right level of heat in every zone.

70. The Mary-go-round

The men stand back-to-back wearing Snuggies upside down to cover their faces. After she's done, she moves on to the next. Round and round and round she goes!

71. The Triple-Decker

Each participant wears a Snuggie, leaving the important bits exposed. It's sixty-nine plus sixty-nine, which adds up to *awesome*. But it's our expectation that once you get started, there would be no math.

72. The Musical Chairs

Many women wear Snuggies, each of a different color. When the music stops, find a seat and thrust yourself onto it.

73. The Hammock

Some days, you just want to relax and take it all in.

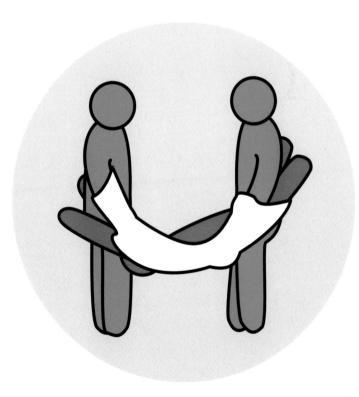

Chapter 7

ADVANCED SNUGGIE SEX: YOU'LL NEED PHYSICAL AND MENTAL BALANCE

Now that you've progressed this far in *The Snuggie Sutra,* your sex life has surely reached heights you never thought possible. You've likely worn out a few Snuggies along the way.

Through the previous chapters, you've already added an incredible variety of Snuggie-based sexual spice into your bedroom arsenal. Now, you're about to discover positions that will stretch your mind and body alike.

While you may have mastered the positions in the earlier chapters with ease, the ones that follow might take more time to master. They may require more strength, more physical prowess, or simply more endurance. But we promise that the extra effort required will pay off.

Relax, and let it happen: We're confident that you're up to the challenge.

And if not, hey, extra pictures of cartoon sex.

74. The Gymnast

She has one leg in the air. He wears the Snuggie, keeping her warm and balanced. Watch your form, stick the landing, and aim for a big finish.

75. The Me Tarzan You Jane

Attach the Snuggie securely to your wall, as a makeshift vine. Her legs go through the sleeves; he holds her up and she supports him. Find out if she's a swinger!

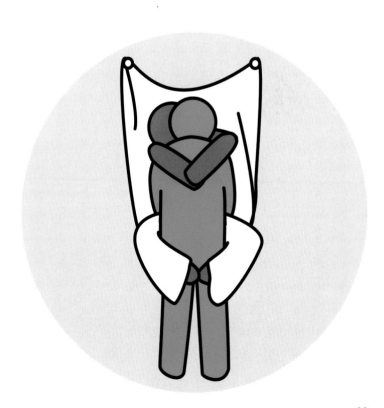

76. The Fleece Hammer

He wears the Snuggie, and holds her up, upsidedown. You know you've nailed it when she's completely swept off her feet.

77. The Pigs in a Blanket

The woman wears the Snuggie on her front, and covers her mate behind her. This may look like spooning, but when you share the Snuggie, it inevitably leads to forking.

78. **The Warm Pretzel**

You each get one arm in the Snuggie, and wrap the remaining fabric around yourselves as you twist together. To be this flexible, your muscles should be warm. The Snuggie's got that covered, as well as all of your major reproductive organs.

79. The Multitaskers

The man sits on the couch using his laptop. He wears the Snuggie on his front. She's reading a great book—perhaps this one. For a busy couple that likes things to happen simultaneously.

80. The Scrimmage Line

She puts one arm through the Snuggie, with the other on the ground for balance. He holds the other end. Before you start the play, make sure your receiver is in position.

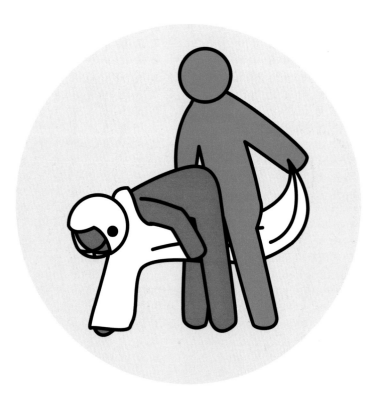

81. The Coffee Cake

The woman lies down on the coffee table. The man sits on the couch wearing the Snuggie. The hostess ensures that everything's served hot for her guests.

82. The Ottoman

The woman wears the Snuggie while sitting on the sofa. If they had the Snuggie back then, the empire might have survived.

83. The Tapestry

He stands behind her as they both put their hands on the wall. Each partner puts both arms through the sleeves of the Snuggie. This wall art is used to tell a story—and this story has a happy ending.

84. The Wheelbarrow

She wears the Snuggie on her front with her hands on the floor; he holds her up using it. Perfect for working her garden.

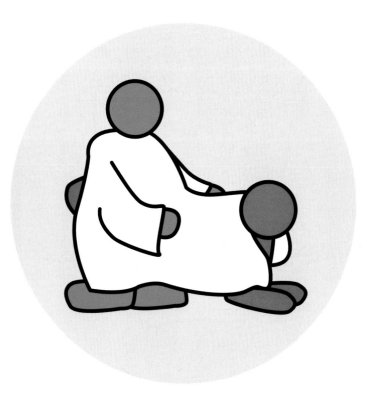

85. The Sleeve It to Beaver

The man wears the Snuggie on his front, aligning himself perectly with one sleeve. Gollygee willikers, that looks like fun.

86. The Boomerang

The woman hangs upside down wearing the Snuggie on her back. You push her away, but she keeps coming back for more.

87. The Physical Challenge

If you can handle this position, you need no further instructions. All the blood will be rushing to her head—and his.

Chapter 8

TEASING, TANTALIZING, AND OTHER SENSUALITY: SUPPLEMENTAL SNUGGIE STIMULATION

You can incorporate your Snuggie into your most intimate moments without intercourse.

On the pages that follow, you'll learn all the right Snuggie moves to turn your partner on with ease.

Of course, many of the Snuggie-based erotic suggestions in this chapter will leave you and your loved one dangerously aroused and ready for action. In that event, feel free to see chapters 1 through 7.

88. The Snuggie Striptease

Wear the Snuggie over your other clothing. As you slowly strip, leave *only* the Snuggie on. Your partner will stare, mouth agape, amazed at how you removed your shirt while keeping your arms firmly in the Snuggie's sleeves.

89. The Mano-a-Snuggie

Don your Snuggie, light some candles, turn on some smooth jazz, and rock your own solo.

90. The Miss Independent

Remember, the Snuggie is machine washable. Go ahead, do unto yourself as you would have others do unto you.

91. The Movie Theater

With your Snuggies on, this is a close, warm, intimate way to watch your favorite adult films (like "Debbie Snuggs Dallas") as a couple. Feel free to shoot your own later.

92. The Doctor Is In

When something ails you, the doctor puts on a Snuggie coat and gives you a thorough examination. Say, "Ahhhhhh."

93. The Surgeon

After the Doctor checks you out, you may need deeper examination. Since the procedure is entirely noninvasive, your recovery time should be quick.

94. The Smock

The Snuggie is worn to keep you clean as you paint a nude portrait of your loved one. You want to be warm while you create your masterpiece. Straddle the line between pornography and art—and anything else you deem worth straddling.

95. The Sideshow

Each of you wears a Snuggie on your back, as you each lie on your side, facing the other. Before the main event, make sure that the bearded lady and the two-ball juggler are warmed up.

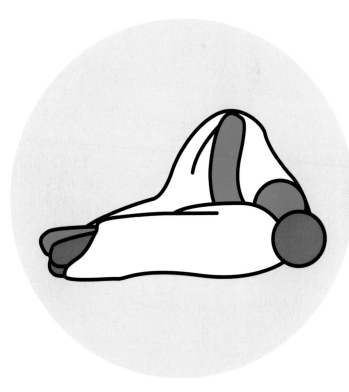

96. The Viewmaster

She hides herself under the blanket. He sneaks peeks through the armholes. The 3-D imagery is so realistic, it's like you could just reach out and touch it.

97. The Hand Puppet

He puts his hand up her Snuggie. The left hand knows exactly what the right hand is doing: Making her jaw drop.

98. Snuggie Massage

The recipient wears the Snuggie. The more she relaxes, the deeper it gets.

99. The Charmer

The woman wears the Snuggie while the man lies on the ground before her. Armed with only the sound of her voice, she can hypnotize the snake to make it rise.

100. The Flasher

The flasher wears the Snuggie on his back. Give her a sneak peek of what's headed her way!

Epilogue

Well, we're spent.

One hundred positions after we started, we can only imagine the sensuous depths your love life has reached courtesy of your Snuggie.

This is the end of *The Snuggie Sutra* the book, but it needn't be the end of The Snuggie Sutra the lifestyle.

Not every inanimate object belongs in your bedroom—even if it happens to have sleeves. But now that you've uncovered the sexiness that a Snuggie can bring, feel free to experiment with other erotic Snuggie use.

FAQ

··

What is *The Snuggie Sutra*?

Really? You got this far into the book, and you're still
confused? You've heard of *The Kama Sutra,* right?
Of course you have; you're clearly a pervert—you
bought a book with fornicating Snuggie-clad cartoon
characters on the cover. Well, *The Snuggie Sutra* is
just like that, a true visual compendium of pleasurable
sex positions. . . . Only ours involves a blanket.
Specifically, a blanket with sleeves.

Do I have to use a Snuggie? Couldn't I just use a bathrobe?

That's like asking if your sex partner has to be human.
We'll leave that decision up to you.

Could I use a Slanket?

Are you serious? Only if you regularly drink RC Cola and intend to use supermarket-brand condoms.

How does the Snuggie react to bodily fluids?

Eagerly.

Will using the Snuggie protect against STDs or pregnancy?

No. Abstaining from sex might. But who are we kidding? You have a Snuggie and a loved one nearby. Sex happens.

I have a great idea for a position to add to *The Snuggie Sutra*.

That's not a question. Try harder.

How can I tell you about my new, kick-ass sexual position that you might want to add to *The Snuggie Sutra*?

Visit our website: http://thesnuggiesutra.com/. The site features web-only positions, other pithy commentary, and a form where you can send us your favorite sexual Snuggie creations. Bear in mind, though, that positions you submit may well become part of our sexual repertoire.

Acknowledgments

We want to thank everyone who said "Wow, that's a really great idea!" when they heard about *The Snuggie Sutra*. Before this was a website or a book, it was a joke told at parties. Thanks for laughing and inspiring us to take it further.

Our deep appreciation to our friends and family, who contribute greatly to our inappropriate, collective sense of humor. We also wish to extend special, exceedingly grateful thanks to Jake and Dana Rubin and Lauren Friedman; you were all extremely patient, always supportive, and immeasurably helpful.

Thanks to all of the online media outlets who made the website a success and are sure to make this book a bestseller.

Special thanks to our agent Rachel Sussman—

and everyone at Zachary Shuster Harmsworth—for making the deal we all wanted, and to our editor Lindsay Sagnette and everyone at St. Martin's Press, for turning a dirty idea into a real live book.

Visit us on the web at http://thesnuggiesutra.com/.

About the Authors

Lex Friedman writes lots of funny things. His comedy music videos have been featured by Yahoo. com and TiVo, and have amassed more than half a million views on YouTube. For a year, Lex wrote and hosted the Web series *The Week in Douchebaggery* on Cracked.com. Lex Twitters, blogs, and occasionally steps away from the computer, only to rush back when he thinks of more sexual positions involving Snuggies. Lex is also frequently published on Macworld.com. He lives in New Jersey with his wife and two young daughters, who may never know of this book's existence. Find Lex online at lexfriedman.com

Megan Morrison lives and works in Washington, D.C., as a graphic designer, and is delighted each day to remember that she actually makes a living at it. Megan enjoys lip gloss, fine liquid dining, and the company of friends and family who said they couldn't be prouder of her upon their first glimpses of tiny cartoon sex drawings tacked up all over her bedroom. Find Megan online at megsammor.com.

We're both always open to your suggestions (and sexual advances) at thesnuggiesutra.com.